ALL BECAUSE OF SAMMYE

Written by:
Amber Parker

Published in the United States of America

ISBN 978-1-960684-03-5 (SC)
ISBN 978-1-960684-02-8 (Ebook)

7Flowers Publications
222 West 6th Street
Suite 400, San Pedro, CA, 90731
fuzzyraccoonlife@gmail.com

Order Information and Rights Permission:

Quantity sales. Special discounts might be available on quantity purchases by corporations, associations, and others. For details, contact the publisher at the address above.

For Book Rights Adaptation and other Rights Permission. Call us at toll-free 1-888-945-8513 or send us an email at admin@stellarliterary.com.

Amber Parker has always loved writing stories. Even as a child, she wrote many short stories. Writing has always been a way for her to express the crazy world around her. Growing up with her adoptive family on a ranch in Texas alongside her three siblings gave her lots of inspiration for her writing.

There were moments when Amber needed some extra help and a time out to learn to process and cope with life, so she moved to Stephenville, Texas, and lived in Sherrwood and Myrtie Foster's Home for Children.

The foster's home was where Amber began searching for what God had planned for her. She returned to the ranch early in her freshman year.

Amber has always felt her purpose was to help others cope and understand where they were in life. She thinks all the trials she endured were to help and taking what she has been through and applying it to help anyone she can.

Amber & her husband Bryan live in Texas, where they raised their two kids. They enjoy family time, pets & being outdoors.

Thank you!
Amber

Nikki and Trixie Squirrel, a pair of lovable creatures who loved each other and the world around them.

The Squirrel family made their home in a forest. Their tree was tall, with thick green leaves and perfect branches for running along and stretching out on warm days.

Inside the tree, there was plenty of room for storing fruits and nuts. They also had a beautiful river right outside the tree

The Squirrels had room to build & paint houses for the other animals that lived in the forest. The Squirrels were busy building birdhouses for the spring.

The Squirrels had finally found a forest of their own, but they were missing one thing: children.

Nikki and Trixie imagined about what it would be like to have children.

Nikki wanted to teach children how to climb the branches so high and build homes for others as he did.

One day, a devastating fire broke out in the forest.
It destroyed many furry families and their homes.
Trees had been burned down and grass had turned black

Nikki and Trixie's home survived, but they were deeply saddened to see the forest they loved damaged. They knew they had to help their neighbors in the forest, whose homes had been damaged.

Nikki and Trixie decided to take a walk to see what the fire had ruined and if they could help anyone. They worked together to gather tools, food, and anything else they could find to help.

As they walk through the forest, they see the Fox family whose house had caved in. Nikki stops to help them to rebuild.

Trixie decides to continue to walk and looks for others who need help.

Trixie had been walking for a long time when she heard someone crying.

15

She followed the sound and discovered a young raccoon, sitting all alone on the bank of the river, covered in ash and soot.

Sammye was covered in ash and smelled of smoke. His silky black mask was soaked in tears. He was a devastating sight to see.

Trixie looked at Sammye's face full of tears, wanting
to comfort him. She said, "Hi, I am Trixie. What is your name?"

With a quiet and Shakey voice,
he replied "My name is Sammye."

"Sammye, the tree is down and still smoking,
and we have to look for safety," Trixie said in a soft voice.

18

Trixie asked Sammye, "Are you okay?" Are you hurt?"
Sammye's voice was filled with tears as he said, "I'm alone."
Sammye had no family after the fire because he was the only
one who survived the falling tree.

Sammye collapsed into Trixie's arms.
As they sat together, her heart was saddened for Sammye.
But Trixie had thought of a plan to help Sammye.

20

Nikki and Trixie had wanted a child for so long. They did not care where he came from as long as he was theirs, and they could love and take care of him.

Sammye looked up at her and Trixie comforted him, "do not worry, you are safe & sound. Come with me to my house while we get you cleaned up." She told him that Nikki would love to meet him & help him.

Holding his small paw, they walked together to the Squirrel's tree. Trixie was thankful their home was safe, and she could offer it to Sammye.

Trixie was eager to get home so Nikki could meet Sammye. She could not wait to share her wishes about Sammye living in their tree and becoming a part of their family.

When they arrive at the Squirrel home, Trixie introduces Sammye to Nikki and shares the news of Sammye losing his family and home. Nikki hugs Sammye after learning all the raccoon had faced that day.

Nikki says to Sammye, "How about I help you start a bath to wash the smoke and dirt off of you while Trixie cooks some snails and chopped nuts and berries for you?"

Sammye thought a bath and hot meal sounded nice. He followed Nikki up to the branches to the bathroom while Trixie went to start preparing the food.

After Sammye had a warm bath to scrub the smoke and dirt off, they ate supper together. Nikki told Trixie & Sammye about how he helped fix the Fox home by cleaning out the ash and finding new wood to build them a new roof.

The sun had gone down and the moon was high in the night sky. They found Sammye some jammies to wear. It was time for the day to end and for them to go to bed.

Nikki & Trixie tucked Sammye in bed and said, "In the morning, we will all talk over breakfast and talk about what we are going to do." They hugged Sammye goodnight and left the room.

The Squirrels were saddened by what had happened to Sammye and they wanted to help. After Sammye was fast asleep, the squirrels talked about how to help him.

The Squirrels agreed to talk to Sammye about staying with them during breakfast.

33

The next day the sun came up, filling the sky with bright colors, and making the room nice and warm. The smell of breakfast cooking woke Sammye.

He crawled out of bed looked out the window and saw the river. As he continues to look out the window, he gets dressed in the clothes that Trixie had cleaned for him. He takes a deep breath, "No Smoke!". He then walked down the branches to the kitchen to join Trixie & Nikki.

Sammye sat at the table where breakfast was waiting for him. As they ate together, the Squirrels said to Sammye, "We would love it if you would stay and live with us in our home and join our family."

Nikki stated he would love Sammye to help fix the forest where the fire had destroyed so much. Sammye wanted to help clean it up.

Trixie stated that she would love to show Sammye how to help gather food to take to other homes since some families have lost all of theirs. Sammye wanted to help right away

They were both overjoyed when Sammye said...

"Yes, I will stay and live here with you.
I want to help work in the forest.
I want to help others."

The Squirrel family was happy now that it included a young raccoon. Nikki and Trixie's big empty tree was filled with love, laughter, and lots of hugs

"ALL BECAUSE OF SAMMYE!"